DATE DUE

OLYMPIC MATH

Working with Percents and Decimals

Greg Roza

PowerMath™

The Rosen Publishing Group's
PowerKids Press™
New York

Published in 2007 by The Rosen Publishing Group, Inc.
29 East 21st Street, New York, NY 10010

Book Design: Michael J. Flynn

Photo Credits: Cover © Dylan Martinez/Reuters/Corbis; p. 5 (torch lighting) © Yannis Behrakis/Reuters/Corbis;
pp. 5 (stadium), 28 © Wally McNamee/Corbis; p. 6 © Historical Picture Archive/Corbis; p. 9 © age fotostock/
SuperStock; pp. 11, 14, 17 (Coubertin inset) © Bettmann/Corbis; p. 13 © Steve Vidler/SuperStock; p. 17
(International Olympic Committee) © Allsport/Getty Images; p. 19 © Time Life Pictures/Getty Images; pp. 21,
23 © Hulton Archive/Getty Images; p. 25 © AFP/Getty Images; p. 26 © GRAF/AFP/Getty Images; p. 27 ©
Steve Powell/Getty Images; p. 29 © Todd Warshaw/Getty Images; p. 30 © Jacques Demarthon/AFP/
Getty Images.

Roza, Greg.
  Olympic math : working with percents and decimals / Greg Roza.
      p. cm. — (Math for the real world)
  Includes index.
  ISBN 1-4042-3352-0 (library binding)
  ISBN 1-4042-6057-9 (pbk.)
  6-pack ISBN 1-4042-6058-7
  1. Fractions—Juvenile literature. 2. Decimal fractions—Juvenile literature. 3. Olympics—Juvenile literature.
4. Olympic games (Ancient)—Juvenile literature. I. Title. II. Series.
  QA117.R85 2006
  513.2'45—dc22

Manufactured in the United States of America

CONTENTS

What Are the Olympic Games?   4

The Olympics of Ancient Greece   7

The Olympic Revival   12

Athens, 1896   18

Paris, 1900   20

Stockholm, 1912   22

Berlin, 1936   24

Lake Placid, 1980   26

Nagano, 1998   28

Back to Athens   30

Glossary   31

Index   32

WHAT ARE THE OLYMPIC GAMES?

During the Olympic Games—a celebration of sportsmanship that now takes place once every 2 years—athletes from around the globe gather to compete in sporting events. The best athletes in each sport win medals, but the Olympics are more than just competitions. The Olympics are a model of goodwill that brings the nations of the world together to honor the concept of global harmony.

There are many symbols associated with the Olympic Games. Most famous are the 5 interlocking rings, which symbolize the 6 continents of the world where people live (North and South America are represented by a single ring). This symbol was first used for the 1920 Olympics in Antwerp, Belgium. The Olympic motto is the Latin phrase *Citius, Altius, Fortius,* which means "faster, higher, stronger." These symbols, along with the concepts of sportsmanship and unity, are essential parts of the Olympic Games.

Math is another important part of the Olympic Games. Without math, we would not be able to keep track of the accomplishments of the athletes. In this book, we will examine the origins of the Olympic Games, as well as some of the most important moments throughout their history, using percents and decimals.

The Olympic flame, first lit during the opening ceremony of the 1928 games in Amsterdam, the Netherlands, is a symbol of knowledge, life, and peace. The flame is lit in Olympia, Greece, the site of the first games over 2,700 years ago. Runners then carry a torch lit by the flame to the site of the current Olympics. The torch lights a cauldron, or giant bowl, which remains lit throughout the games.

THE OLYMPICS OF ANCIENT GREECE

The ancient Greeks believed that a well-educated person was fit in all areas of life. The training required to compete in athletic events involved patience and endurance, qualities highly valued in Greek society. Victory in an athletic event was a sign of mental, physical, moral, and spiritual excellence.

Winning an athletic event brought great fame not only to the athlete and his family, but also to the Greek city that he represented at the games. Ancient Greek culture highly valued heroes of many kinds, and athletic champions were often treated like heroes. The men who were victorious at the Olympics and other festivals were thought to be blessed by the gods. The athletes who won multiple competitions were renowned for their great athletic abilities. They were often **immortalized** by statues, paintings, poems, and legends that lasted for centuries. These legends sometimes changed over time, lending superhuman qualities to the men they honored. Just like the heroes of ancient legends—such as Odysseus, hero of the Greek stories the *Iliad* and the *Odyssey*—Olympic champions hoped to attain fame and glory that lasted long after they had passed away.

The ancient Olympic games took place in Olympia, Greece. The ancient Greeks believed that mythical gods and heroes once held athletic games in this location. Zeus was the king of the Greek gods. The Temple of Zeus in Olympia—now in ruins—once housed one of the Seven Wonders of the Ancient World, the statue of Zeus at Olympia. This is an artist's depiction of how the statue may have looked.

Greece's history of national sporting festivals dates back to as early as 1200 B.C. Historians believe competitions were originally staged to honor the dead. Later, athletic games were held during religious festivals to honor Greek gods.

The first recorded Olympic Games were held in 776 B.C. In the fifth century B.C., a Greek writer named Hippias of Elis compiled the first list of Olympic champions. He and other historians left a record of the Olympic winners from 776 B.C. until A.D. 369. The original Olympic Games had only 1 event. The *stade*, or *stadion*, was a 210-yard race. Over the years, longer races and other events—such as boxing, wrestling, **pentathlon**, horse racing, chariot racing, racing in armor, and even trumpeting—were added.

The men who served as judges for the Olympic Games in ancient Greece were known as the *hellanodikai* (Greek for "the judges of the Greeks"). These judges also organized events and trained athletes. During the games, the judges wore robes of purple, a royal color, in honor of their important roles.

This track in Olympia, Greece—on which the *stade* may have been run—dates back to the fifth century B.C. A *stade* or *stadion* was equal to 210 yards. In 720 B.C., a race was added to the games that was the length of 24 *stade*s. How many miles long was this race? To find the answer, you need to know that there are 1,760 yards in a mile.

First, find out how many yards are in the longer race by multiplying 210 yards by 24 *stade*s.

```
    210  yards (1 stade)
  x  24  stades
    840
  + 420
  5,040  yards
```

The longer race was a total of 5,040 yards.

Now, divide the number of yards in the longer race by the number of yards in a mile. Round your answer to the nearest tenth.

```
              2.86 miles
1,760 ) 5,040.00
       -3 520
        1 5200
       -1 4080
          11200
         -10560
            640
```

The longer race was about 2.9 miles long.

Athletics were an important part of life for all ancient Greeks, although only Greek men could participate in the Olympic Games. The Olympics eventually became a sacred national festival. Greek **city-states** even halted their battles in honor of the games. Greek athletes competed for honor and fame, not for material gains. However, Olympic winners were often excused from paying taxes and sometimes got free meals for life.

After Greece was conquered by Macedonia in 338 B.C., the Olympic Games were attended by athletes from a larger area. Eventually the focus of the games shifted from religious ceremony to physical competition. Victory in events was now considered a display of athletic excellence rather than a blessing from the gods.

Greece was conquered by Rome in 146 B.C. Roman nobility did not participate in athletic competitions but enjoyed watching and betting on them. Games were often staged to honor the Roman emperor. Athletes no longer took pride in competing as they once had. In fact, most competitors at the Olympic Games were slaves or **gladiators**. In A.D. 393, the Christian Roman emperor Theodosius I declared all **pagan** rituals illegal. After nearly 1,200 years, the Olympic Games were abandoned.

The Olympic Games—shown here in Roman times—were held once every 4 years, a unit of time the Greeks called an olympiad. We have records of the Olympic games from 776 B.C. until A.D. 392, a total of 1,168 years. How many olympiads are there in 1,168 years? What percent of 1,168 is that number?

To answer the first question, we need to divide 1,168 years by 4 to get the number of olympiads that occurred during that period of time.

$$\begin{array}{r} 292 \\ 4{\overline{\smash{\big)}\,1{,}168}} \end{array}$$

There are 292 olympiads in 1,168 years.

Now we need to find out what percent of 1,168 is represented by 292. To do this, we need to set up a proportion. A proportion is a comparison of equal ratios. Let t equal the percent you want to find.

$$\frac{t}{100} = \frac{292}{1{,}168}$$

To find t, you first cross multiply. Then divide to find the answer.

$$1{,}168 \times t = 292 \times 100$$

$$1{,}168t = 29{,}200$$

$$\frac{1{,}168t}{1{,}168} = \frac{29{,}200}{1{,}168}$$

$$\begin{array}{r} 25 \\ 1{,}168{\overline{\smash{\big)}\,29{,}200}} \\ \underline{-23\,36} \\ 5\,840 \\ \underline{-5\,840} \\ 0 \end{array}$$

$t = 25\%$

The number of olympiads (292) is 25% of 1,168.

Perhaps you have noticed an easier way to solve this problem. In the caption, we were told that the Olympic Games were held 1 out of every 4 years. One out of 4, or $\frac{1}{4}$, is 25%.

THE OLYMPIC REVIVAL

In 1829, Greece became a free nation for the first time since 338 B.C. Russia, Britain, and France helped Greece win its independence from the **Ottoman Empire**, which had ruled the country since the 1450s. Archaeologists now began to explore Greece. They uncovered many ancient towns and buildings, including the stadiums and temples at Olympia. This renewed the world's interest in ancient Greece and the Olympic Games.

There were several attempts to reestablish organized athletic games in Greece in the mid-1800s. Beginning in 1859, a wealthy businessman and landowner named Evangelis Zappas helped to organize athletic games. He was influenced by Greek poet Alexandros Soutsos, who had written a poem about a revival of the ancient Olympic Games. The focus of Zappas's games was not simply athletic competitions, but also industrial and agricultural exhibits. The Zappas games, held in 1859, 1870, 1875, and 1889, were often poorly organized and eventually ceased. However, the modern Olympic Games borrowed many things from them, including awarding medals as prizes to winners and holding special ceremonies before and after the games.

Evangelis Zappas provided much money for the excavation and restoration of ancient Greek buildings, including the Panathenian, also known as the Olympic Stadium, in Athens, Greece. It is believed that the original stadium had room for about 50,000 spectators. Today, marble benches allow about 40% more people to watch events. Approximately how many spectators can watch events at the Panathenian today?

To solve this problem, let's set up another proportion. We need to find 40% of 50,000. Let p equal the amount we want to find.

$$\frac{p}{50,000} = \frac{40}{100}$$

Cross multiply and solve for p.

$$100p = 40 \times 50,000$$

$$\begin{array}{r} 50,000 \\ \times \quad\;\; 40 \\ \hline 2,000,000 \end{array}$$

$$\frac{100p}{100} = \frac{2,000,000}{100}$$

$$p = 20,000$$

Then we need to add that amount to 50,000 to find the total number of spectators that can fit in the stadium.

$$\begin{array}{r} 50,000 \\ + \; 20,000 \\ \hline 70,000 \end{array}$$

Today, about 70,000 people can watch events at the Panathenian.

THE PANATHENIAN

13

BARON PIERRE
DE COUBERTIN

Another man who influenced the revival of the Olympic Games was a French educator named Baron Pierre de Coubertin. In the late 1800s, Coubertin saw the need for change in French education. Between the ages of 17 and 24, he traveled to England and America to observe their educational practices. Coubertin decided that the French education system lacked the character-building qualities of athletics that he saw in the education systems of England and America.

After returning to France, Coubertin wrote several articles and made speeches praising the English and American educational systems for their emphasis on athletic competition. His ideas were not widely accepted at first. Many French educators believed that athletics distracted students from other lessons. Much like the ancient Greeks, however, Coubertin believed that athletics were a healthy way to strengthen a person physically, mentally, and spiritually.

Upon learning of new archaeological discoveries in Greece, Coubertin thought it might be possible to hold athletic competitions similar to those held during ancient Greek times. He believed athletic competition could help strengthen youthful minds and bring the countries of the world together at the same time.

 Coubertin was an enthusiastic sportsman. He enjoyed participating in athletic activities such as boxing, fencing, horse riding, and rowing.

In 1887, Coubertin founded the Union of French Athletic Sports Clubs, hoping to spread his interest in international sporting events to others around the globe. He believed that developing an enthusiasm for athletics would promote pride in the French people and culture. He began to receive support for his ideas.

In 1894, Coubertin organized a conference in Paris, France, called the International Congress on **Amateurism**. The conference was attended by 79 sports experts from 9 countries, including France, Britain, and the United States. Coubertin raised the issue of establishing an international athletic competition.

During the meeting, the members established the International Olympic Committee, or IOC. They also made plans to stage the first modern Olympic Games in Athens, Greece, in 1896. Coubertin served as the committee's first secretary general. In 1896, he became chairman of the committee, a position he held for 29 years. During that time, Coubertin managed the majority of the committee's business and continued to promote the games. Today, Coubertin is known as the father of the modern Olympic Games.

This photograph from 1896 shows the first IOC. Coubertin is seated on the left side of the table.

BARON PIERRE
DE COUBERTIN

ATHENS, 1896

The first modern Olympic Games were held in Athens, Greece, in the summer of 1896. First-place winners received a silver medal and an olive wreath. Second-place winners received a copper medal and a **laurel wreath**. Both received official certificates.

Most contestants were from Greece. For Greeks, the marathon—a 40-kilometer (24.8-mile) race—was the most important event of the 1896 games. A 24-year-old shepherd named Spyridon Louis ran the race in shoes that were given to him by the people of his village. The race began in Marathon, Greece, and ended in the Olympic stadium in Athens. Louis entered the stadium 7 minutes ahead of the next runner. Greeks chanted his name and threw flowers onto the track where he crossed the finish line. He finished the race in 2 hours and 59 minutes.

As in the ancient Olympic Games, women were not allowed to participate. A Greek woman named Stamata Revithi ran her own marathon at the first Olympic Games the day after the men had run the official race. Although she was not allowed to enter the stadium at the end of her race, Revithi finished the marathon in about 5 hours and 30 minutes.

ꝏꝏꝏ

A pie chart is a graph that shows percents of a whole. The pie chart at the top of page 19 shows the percents of athletes who came in first place based on their country. There were a total of 43 events during the 1896 Olympics. Use the pie chart to find out how many events were won by Greek athletes.

First-place Winners at the 1896 Olympics

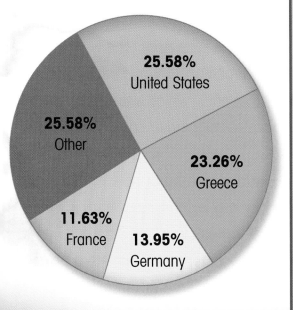

- **25.58%** United States
- **25.58%** Other
- **23.26%** Greece
- **11.63%** France
- **13.95%** Germany

To find out how many events were won by Greek athletes, we need to find 23.26% of 43 total events. To do this, we first need to change 23.26% to a decimal.

The number 23.26% means 23.26 out of 100, or $\frac{23.26}{100}$. Divide 23.26 by 100 to get 0.2326.

Now, multiply 0.2326 by 43. Round your answer to the nearest whole number.

$$
\begin{array}{r}
0.2326 \\
\times \quad 43 \\
\hline
0\ 6978 \\
+\ 9\ 304 \\
\hline
10.0018
\end{array}
$$

Greek athletes won a total of 10 events at the 1896 Olympics.

How many events did the United States win? How many events did Germany and France win altogether? Use the method shown above to find your answers.

THE PANATHENIAN, ATHENS
OLYMPIC GAMES, 1896

Paris, 1900

The 1900 Olympic Games were held in Paris, France. The events were spread out over a 5-month period, and attendance was poor. The Paris Olympics were held as part of the Universal Exposition, a world's fair. The Universal Exposition featured its own sporting events, which were held at the same time as the Olympic events. Some athletes may have competed in events for both competitions.

The 1896 Olympics had been protested by some groups who felt that women should be included in the events. They argued that the Olympic Games could not truly stand for international harmony unless women were allowed to compete. The 1900 Olympics were the first to include female athletes. Women competed in croquet, lawn tennis, and golf. The first female Olympic champion was Charlotte Cooper of Great Britain, who won first place in women's singles tennis. The top 3 finishers in women's golf were from the United States. Margaret Abbott took first place.

A total of 975 male athletes competed at the 1900 Olympics; 22 female athletes also competed. What percent of the athletes at the 1900 Olympics were female?

To find out, we first need to know the total number of athletes.

$$\begin{array}{r} 975 \text{ men} \\ + \quad 22 \text{ women} \\ \hline 997 \text{ total athletes} \end{array}$$

Now we need to find out what percent of 997 is represented by 22. To do this, we need to set up a proportion. Cross multiply and solve for the percent, n

$$\frac{n}{100} = \frac{22}{997}$$

$$997n = 2{,}200$$

Divide by 997. Round your answer to the nearest tenth.

$$\begin{array}{r} 2.20 \\ 997\overline{)2{,}200.00} \\ -1\,994 \\ \hline 206\,0 \\ -199\,4 \\ \hline 6\,60 \\ -0\,00 \\ \hline 6\,60 \end{array}$$

$n = 2.2\%$

Only 2.2% of the athletes at the 1900 Olympics were female.

CHARLOTTE COOPER

21

STOCKHOLM, 1912

The Olympic Games in 1912 were held in Stockholm, Sweden, and were the first to feature electronic timers and loudspeakers. Women's swimming and diving were added to the competition. The longest race in Olympic history—the cycling road race—was held during the 1912 games. It was 199 miles (320 km) long.

The big story of the 1912 Olympics was the athletic achievements of Native American Jim Thorpe. Thorpe, considered one of the best athletes of the twentieth century, would later become famous in the United States for his excellence in professional baseball and professional football. Thorpe was the first athlete to win both the **decathlon** and the pentathlon, setting world records in these events. At the awards ceremony, the king of Sweden told Thorpe, "Sir, you are the greatest athlete in the world."

One year later, the IOC took Thorpe's medals away from him after discovering that he had received a salary of $15 a week playing minor league baseball. At this time, paid professionals were not allowed to compete in the Olympics. In 1982, the IOC overruled the judgment and returned the medals to Thorpe's family. Thorpe is still considered one of the greatest athletes ever to participate in the Olympic Games.

ⓒⓒⓒ

A total of 103 gold medals were awarded at the 1912 Olympic Games. The United States won the most with 25, followed closely by Sweden with 24. Which of the following numbers is closest to the percent of the total number of gold medals won by the United States and Sweden combined: 51.92%, 49.04%, or 47.57%?

▶

First, add 25 and 24 to find out how many gold medals the 2 countries won altogether.

$$\begin{array}{r} 25 \\ + \ 24 \\ \hline 49 \end{array}$$

Now set up a proportion to find out what percent of 103 is represented by 49. Solve for the percent, g. Round your answer to the nearest hundredth.

$$\frac{g}{100} = \frac{49}{103}$$

$$103g = 4{,}900$$

$$\begin{array}{r} 47.572 \\ 103\overline{)4{,}900.000} \\ -4\,12 \\ \hline 780 \\ -721 \\ \hline 59\,0 \\ -515 \\ \hline 7\,50 \\ -7\,21 \\ \hline 290 \\ -206 \\ \hline 84 \end{array}$$

$$g = 47.57\%$$

The United States and Sweden won approximately 47.57%—almost half—of the gold medals at the 1912 Olympics.

BERLIN, 1936

The 1936 Olympics were the first games to be shown on television and the first to feature the now-famous Olympic torch relay. That year, the games were held in Berlin, Germany. Germany was under the control of Adolf Hitler and the **Nazi** party. Hitler wanted to prove to the world that German athletes were superior to athletes of other nationalities and races. Many countries expressed concerns over the decision to hold the games in Berlin, but the games went on as planned. In fact, they were the largest Olympic Games up to that time, involving 49 nations and 3,963 athletes.

The most remarkable story of the 1936 Olympics was African American track-and-field star Jesse Owens. During the games, Owens tied the world record for the 100-meter dash and set Olympic records in the 200-meter dash and the long jump. His relay team set a new Olympic and world record in the 400-meter relay. By the end of the Olympic games, every nation was cheering for Owens.

The 1936 Olympics also featured American Marjorie Gestring, who won the gold medal in diving at the age of 13. Gestring is the youngest athlete to win a gold medal in a summer Olympic event.

Jesse Owens set the Olympic record in the 200-meter dash on August 5, 1936, by running the race in 20.7 seconds. The silver medalist, American Mack Robinson, ran the race in 21.1 seconds. The bronze medalist, Martinus Osendarp of the Netherlands, ran the race in 21.3 seconds. Rounding to the nearest hundredth, what is the average of these 3 numbers?

To find the average, we first need to find the sum of the 3 numbers.

```
   20.7
   21.1
+  21.3
   63.1
```

Now divide 63.1 by 3. Round the answer to the nearest hundredth.

```
       21.033
   3 ) 63.100
      -6
       03
       -3
        010
        - 9
          10
         - 9
           1
```

The average of the 3 numbers is 21.03 seconds.

JESSE OWENS

LAKE PLACID, 1980

HANNI WENZEL

In 1980, the Winter Olympics were held in Lake Placid, New York. It was the first time that man-made snow was used for the Olympic Games. That year, skier Hanni Wenzel from the tiny European country of Liechtenstein won the silver medal in women's downhill skiing and gold medals in the women's **slalom** and giant slalom. This made Liechtenstein the smallest country to have a gold-medal winner. Wenzel's brother Andreas also won a silver medal in men's downhill skiing.

American skater Eric Heiden won all 5 men's speed-skating events, setting an Olympic record in every race. Heiden was the first athlete in Olympic history to win 5 gold medals at the same Olympic Games.

The other big story of the 1980 Olympics was the American men's hockey team. The American team was not expected to play well and had been rated seventh out of the 12 teams competing. They had suffered an embarrassing 10-3 defeat in an exhibition game against the dominant Soviet team the week before the Olympics. The 2 teams met once again in the **semifinals**. The Americans beat the Soviets 4-3 and then went on to win the gold-medal round against Finland.

During the 1980 Olympics, a total of 115 medals were awarded. The United States won approximately 10.43% of the medals. The number of medals that Liechtenstein won was 33.33% of the number the United States won. How many medals did the United States win? How many did Liechtenstein win?

To find out how many medals the United States won, you can set up a proportion as in previous examples. Another way to find the answer is to multiply 10.43% by 115. First, change 10.43 into a decimal by dividing by 100 to get 0.1043. Now multiply. Round your answer to the nearest whole number.

```
    0.1043
  x    115
    5215
    1043
 +1043
   11.9945
```

The United States won 12 medals.

To find out how many medals Liechtenstein won, multiply 33.33%, or 0.3333, by 12. Round your answer to the nearest whole number.

```
    0.3333
  x     12
    6666
 +3 333
    3.9996
```

Liechtenstein won 4 medals during the 1980 Winter Olympics.

NAGANO, 1998

During the 1998 Winter Olympics in Nagano, Japan, snowboarding, **curling**, and women's ice hockey were added to the program. It was also the first year that professional ice hockey athletes were allowed to compete. The men's hockey team from the Czech Republic stunned the world by beating the Russian team to win the gold medal. The U.S. women's hockey team went undefeated to win the first gold medal ever awarded in women's Olympic hockey.

American figure skater Tara Lipinski was just 15 when she competed in Nagano. Lipinski took the gold medal, making her the youngest athlete ever to win a gold medal at a Winter Olympic Games.

Norwegian cross-country skier Bjorn Daehlie won 3 gold medals in Nagano, bringing his total Olympic medal count to 12. Daehlie is the only winter athlete to win 8 gold medals and 12 total medals.

TARA LIPINSKI

At the 1998 Olympics, Bjorn Daehlie won the gold in the men's 50-kilometer (31-mile) cross-country skiing race. He described that race as the hardest in his career. Daehlie crossed the finish line 7,508.2 seconds after starting the race. Rounding to the nearest hundredth, how many minutes is that? Rounding to the nearest hundredth, how many hours is that?

Since there are 60 seconds in 1 minute, divide 7,508.2 seconds by 60 to find the number of minutes. Round the answer to the nearest hundredth.

```
        125.136
60 ) 7,508.200
    - 60
      150
     -120
       308
      - 300
          8 2
         -6 0
          2 20
         -1 80
            400
           - 360
              40
```

It took Daehlie approximately 125.14 minutes to finish the race.

Since there are 60 minutes in every hour, divide the number of minutes by 60 to find the number of hours. Round the answer to the nearest hundredth.

```
        2.085
60 ) 125.140
    - 120
        5 1
       - 0 0
        5 14
       - 4 80
          340
         - 300
           40
```

It took Daehlie approximately 2.09 hours to cross the finish line.

BJORN DAEHLIE

BACK TO ATHENS

In the summer of 2004, the Summer Olympic Games were once again held in Athens, Greece. For the people of Greece, hosting the games in the country where they originated nearly 2,500 years ago was a source of great pride.

Women's wrestling made its first appearance at the 2004 Summer Olympics, and Irini Merleni of the Ukraine was the first gold-medal winner in that sport. The U.S. women's soccer team, led by soccer superstar Mia Hamm, won the gold medal. The U.S. women's softball team also won the gold medal and outscored their opponents 5 to 1. Americans Kerri Walsh and Misty May won the gold medal in beach volleyball.

Perhaps the most exciting story of the 2004 Olympic Games was U.S. swimmer Michael Phelps. At age 19, Phelps won 6 gold medals and a total of 8 medals, tying the record for the most medals won at a single Olympics.

For over 100 years, the modern Olympics have been entertaining and uniting people all over the world. As the Olympic Games continue to bring people from different countries together through athletic competition, the math concepts of percents and decimals will continue to play a vital role.

GLOSSARY

amateurism (AA-muh-chur-ih-zuhm) Engaging in athletics for fun and fulfillment, rather than as a job.

city-state (SIH-tee–STAYT) An independent state consisting of a city and the surrounding territory.

curling (KUHR-ling) A game in which teams slide stones over ice toward a target circle.

decathlon (dih-KATH-lahn) A sporting contest that is made up of 10 events: 100-meter, 400-meter, and 1500-meter races; 110-meter high hurdles; javelin throw; discus throw; shot put; pole vault; high jump; and long jump.

gladiator (GLA-dee-ay-tuhr) In ancient Rome, a person forced to participate in a public fight or sporting event, often to the death.

immortalize (ih-MOHR-tuh-lyz) To cause someone to be remembered by others long after death.

laurel wreath (LOHR-uhl REETH) A wreath made from the branches of a shrub with small yellow flowers, evergreen leaves, and black berries. The ancient Greeks awarded Olympic winners a crown made of laurel branches.

Nazi (NAHT-see) The German political party controlling Germany from 1933 to 1945 under Adolf Hitler.

Ottoman Empire (AH-tuh-muhn EHM-pyr) A great empire ruled by nomadic Turkish tribes that lasted from about 1300 until 1922.

pagan (PAY-guhn) In the ancient world, a non-Christian who believed in the existence of many gods.

pentathlon (pen-TATH-lahn) A sporting contest that is made up of 5 events: a freestyle swim over 200 meters, 3,000-meter cross-country run, 350- to 450-meter 15-jump horse race, fencing, and target shooting.

semifinal (seh-mee-FY-nuhl) The next-to-the-last round in an athletic tournament.

slalom (SLAH-luhm) A downhill skiing race where the skiers must zigzag around a series of flags on their way to the finish line.

INDEX

A

Abbott, Margaret, 20
Athens, Greece, 16, 18, 30

B

Berlin, Germany, 24

C

Cooper, Charlotte, 20
Coubertin, Baron Pierre de, 15, 16

D

Daehlie, Bjorn, 28, 29

G

Gestring, Marjorie, 24

H

Hamm, Mia, 30
Heiden, Eric, 26
hellanodikai, 8
Hippias of Elis, 8
Hitler, Adolf, 24
hockey, 26, 28

I

International Congress on Amateurism, 16
International Olympic Committee (IOC),
        16, 22

L

Lake Placid, New York, 26
Lipinski, Tara, 28
Louis, Spyridon, 18

M

May, Misty, 30
Merleni, Irini, 30

N

Nagano, Japan, 28

O

Olympia, 12
Owens, Jesse, 24

P

Paris, France, 16, 20
Phelps, Michael, 30

R

Revithi, Stamata, 18

S

Soutsos, Alexandros, 12
stade (s), 8, 9
Stockholm, Sweden, 22

T

Thorpe, Jim, 22

U

Universal Exposition, 20

W

Walsh, Kerri, 30
Wenzel, Hanni, 26

Z

Zappas, Evangelis, 12